Real-World

Problem Solving

Graphic Novels

BOOK 2

McGraw Hill Glencoe

New York, New York
Columbus, Ohio
Chicago, Illinois
Woodland Hills, California

Illustrators: *Greg Lawhun, Wayno, Michael McParlane, Mark Ricketts, Shane McDermott, Joel Priddy, Scott Rolfs, Pat Lewis, Jim Callahan*

Mc Graw Hill Glencoe

The McGraw·Hill Companies

Send all inquiries to:

Glencoe/McGraw-Hill
8787 Orion Place
Columbus, OH 43240-4027

ISBN: 978-0-07-878294-7
MHID: 0-07-878294-5

Printed in the United States of America.

9 10 045 15 14 13 12 11 10 09

TABLE of CONTENTS

Letter to the Teacher iv

Teaching Strategies and Answers v

Number Sense

1 Compare Rational Numbers: Game Room 1
2 Add Integers: Fourth and Long 4
3 Unit Rates: Tracking Time 5
Practice On Your Own 6

Algebraic Thinking

1 Unit Costs: Mister Lincoln Goes Surfing 7
2 Percent: Wits for Tips 10
3 Write Equations: Cell Phone Surprise 11
Practice On Your Own 12

Geometry

1 Similar Figures: A Tall Story 13
2 Reflections: Floor Show 16
3 Quadrilaterals: Right Angles? 17
Practice On Your Own 18

Measurement

1 Volume of Cylinders: Find a Better Deal 19
2 Volume of Prisms and Cylinders: Shipping Shenanigans 22
3 Area of Polygons: Paint by Number 23
Practice On Your Own 24

Statistics and Probability

1 Probability: Lucky Count 25
2 Independent Events: Sibling Probabilities 28
3 Measures of Central Tendency: Hot! Hot! Hot? 29
Practice On Your Own 30

Mathematical Reasoning

1 Four-Step Plan: To DVD, or not to DVD, that is the Question 31
2 Make an Organized List: Cinema Dilemma 34
3 Look for a Pattern: Practice Makes Perfect 35
Practice On Your Own 36

LETTER to the TEACHER

USING GRAPHIC NOVELS:
Popular Culture and Mathematics Interact

Graphic novels represent a significant segment of the literary market for adolescents and young adults. They are amazingly diverse, both in terms of their content and usefulness. Graphic novels are exactly what teens are looking for—they are motivating, engaging, challenging, and interesting. They allow teachers to enter the youth culture and students to bring their "out of school" experiences into the classroom.

Graphic novels have also been used effectively with students with disabilities, struggling readers, and English learners. One of the theories behind the use of graphic novels for struggling adolescents focuses on the fact that the graphic novel presents complex ideas that are interesting and engaging for adolescents, while reducing the text or reading demands.

However, graphic novels are motivating and engaging for *all* students. They allow us to differentiate our instruction and provide universal access to the curriculum. We hope you'll find the graphic novels in this book useful as you engage your students in the study of mathematics and problem-solving.

Sincerely,
Douglas Fisher & Nancy Frey

Douglas Fisher, Ph.D.
Professor
San Diego State University

Nancy Frey, Ph.D.
Associate Professor
San Diego State University

TEACHING STRATEGIES and ANSWERS

Graphic Novels in the Classroom

As we have noted, graphic novels are an excellent adjunct text. While they cannot and should not replace reading or the core, standards-based textbook, they can be effectively used to build students' background knowledge, to motivate students, to provide a different access route to the content, and to allow students to check and review their work.

Mathematical problem solving is presented in graphic novel format. The novels contain real-world problems for each of the following mathematical content strands: Number Sense, Algebraic Thinking, Geometry, Measurement, Statistics and Probability, and Mathematical Reasoning.

- The first graphic novel that appears in each content strand describes a real-world problem that is solved in graphic novel format.
- The second and third graphic novels that appear in each content strand are left to the reader to formulate the solution.
- Finally, there are additional problems for students to practice on their own.

Teaching Strategies

1. **Previewing Content** You can use a graphic novel as a lesson preview to activate background and prior knowledge. For example, you may display a graphic novel on the overhead projector and discuss it with the class. By doing so, you may provide students with advance information that they will read later in the book. Alternatively, you may display the graphic novel and invite students, in pairs or groups, to share their thinking with one another. Regardless of the approach, the goal is to activate students' interest and background knowledge in advance of the reading.

2. **Narrative Writing** Use the second and third graphic novels from each content strand and ask students to solve the posed problem in graphic novel format. Students should be encouraged to create character dialogue and complete the story line detailing their solution. Another alternative is to provide students with the first two pages of the first graphic novel and ask students to complete the story line with the solution to the problem posed. Not only does this engage students in thinking about the content, but it also provides you with some assessment information. Based on the dialogue that the students create of their solution, you'll understand what they already know, what they misunderstand, and what they do not yet know.

3. **Reviewing Content** In addition to narrative summaries, graphic novels can also be used for content review. While there are many reasons to review content—such as preparing for a test—graphic novels are especially useful for providing students with a review of past chapters. You can use a graphic novel from a previous chapter to review its major concepts.

4. **Analysis** In the analysis approach, students read the graphic novel to try to understand the main point the author is making. This approach is particularly useful after students have covered the content in their textbook. Encouraging students to pose questions about the text will help to uncover the main points. For example:

    - Why did the author choose this real-world situation to present this concept we have studied? What are some other real-world situations that can be used to present this concept?
    - What does the graphic novel tell me about this concept we have studied?

    Have students write a few sentences answering these questions. Then have them summarize what they believe is the main point of the graphic novel.

5. **Visualizing** Have your students skim over the exercises in the chapter you are working on or the Practice On Your Own pages. The student should then pick one exercise and create their own graphic representation about it. Another option would be to use other forms of multimedia for their topic. Students could take pictures, make a computer slide-show presentation, make a video, or create a song.

These are just some of the many uses of graphic novels. As you introduce them into your class, you may discover more ways to use them to engage your students in a new method of learning while exercising the multiple literacies that your students already possess. We welcome you to the world of learning through graphic novels!

References

Cary, S. (2004). Going graphic: *Comics at work in the multilingual classroom.* Portsmouth, NH: Heinemann.

Fisher, D., & Frey, N. (2004). *Improving adolescent literacy: Strategies at work.* Upper Saddle River, NJ: Merrill Education.

Frey, N., & Fisher, D. (2004). Using graphic novels, anime, and the Internet in an urban high school. *English Journal, 93*(3), 19–25.

Gorman, M. (2002). What teens want: Thirty graphic novels you can't live without. *School Library Journal, 48*(8), 42–47.

Schwarz, G. (2002a). Graphic novels for diverse needs: Engaging reluctant and curious readers. *ALAN Review, 30*(1), 54–57.

Schwarz, G. (2002b). Graphic novels for multiple literacies. *Journal of Adolescent & Adult Literacy, 46,* 262–265.

Schwarz, G. (2004). Graphic novels: Multiple cultures and multiple literacies. *Thinking Classroom, 5*(4), 17–24.

ANSWERS

Number Sense

Add Integers: Fourth and Long, page 4

On the first down, the team lost 10 yards. Represent this loss as a negative integer, -10.

On the second down, the team gained 15 yards. Represent this gain as a positive integer, 15.

On the third down, the team lost 12 yards. Represent this loss as a negative integer, -12.

On the fourth down, the team gained 23 yards. Represent this gain as a positive integer, 23.

Find the sum of the integers to find the total yards gained for the four downs.
$(-10) + 15 + (-12) + 23 = 16$

They gained a total of 16 yards. Since $16 > 10$, the Tigers get to keep the ball.

Unit Rates: Tracking Time, page 5

To find how long it would take each of them to run 220 yards at the same rate that they each ran 100 yards, first find each unit rate. To do this, divide the time it took to run 100 yards by the number of yards, 100. To divide by 100, move the decimal point two places to the left.

Malcolm's unit rate: 11.4 seconds $\div$ 100 yards $=$ 0.114 seconds per yard.

Candida's unit rate: 12.7 seconds $\div$ 100 yards $=$ 0.127 seconds per yard.

Next, multiply each unit rate by 220 to find the time it would take each of them, at this rate, to run 220 yards.

Since $0.114 \times 220 = 25.08$, it would take Malcolm 25.08 seconds to run the 220-yard dash at this rate.

Since $0.127 \times 220 = 27.94$, it would take Candida 27.94 seconds to run the 220-yard dash at this rate.

Practice On Your Own, page 6

1. D **2.** G **3.** B **4.** H **5.** A **6.** J **7.** B **8.** F

Algebraic Thinking

Percent: Wits for Tips, page 10

To estimate 20% of the restaurant bill, first write 20% as a decimal, 0.2. Then multiply mentally by the approximate amount of the bill. Since $18.95 ≈ $19.00, mentally find 20% of $19.00. To find 20% of $19.00, find 0.2 × $19.00 mentally.

Find 10% of $19.00, or $1.90. Since 20% is twice 10%, 20% of $19.00 is twice the amount $1.90, or $3.80.

So, the amount of the tip should be about $3.80.

Write Equations: Cell Phone Surprise, page 11

First, write an equation representing this situation. Let *x* represent the number of overtime minutes Trevor used on his cell phone.

$$0.45x + 34.95 = 44.85$$

$$-34.95 \quad -34.95 \quad \text{Subtract 34.95 from each side.}$$

$$0.45x = 9.90 \quad \text{Simplify.}$$

$$\frac{0.45x}{0.45} = \frac{9.90}{0.45} \quad \text{Divide each side by 0.45.}$$

$$x = 22 \quad \text{Simplify.}$$

So, Trevor used 22 overtime minutes.

Practice On Your Own, page 12

1. B **2.** F **3.** B **4.** J **5.** B **6.** H

Geometry

Reflections: Floor Show, page 16

The total design can be found by a series of reflections.

First, reflect the design in the 6- by 6-tile layout across the *y*-axis to obtain a 6- by 12-tile layout.

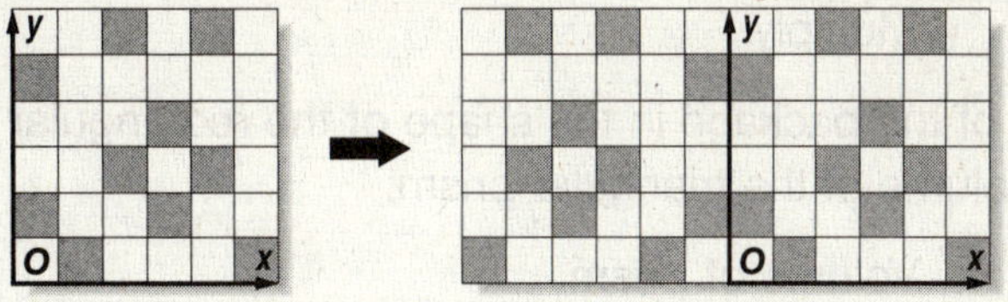

Next, reflect the design in the 6- by 12-tile layout across the *x*-axis to obtain a 12- by 12-tile layout, which is the total design.

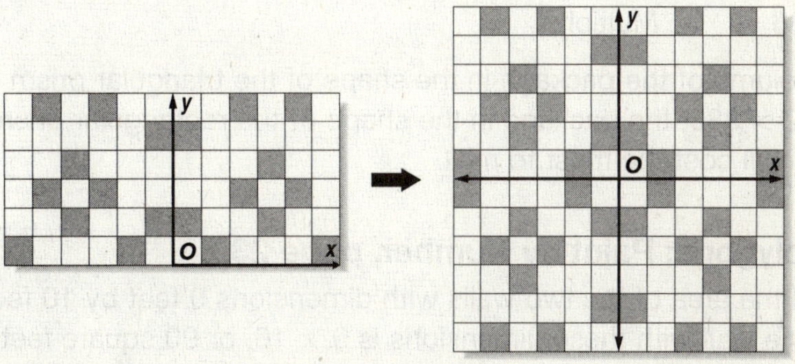

Quadrilaterals: Right Angles?, page 17

Since a rectangle is a special kind of a parallelogram, it has all of the properties of a parallelogram. In addition, a rectangle has four right angles. The following diagram shows how several kinds of parallelograms are related.

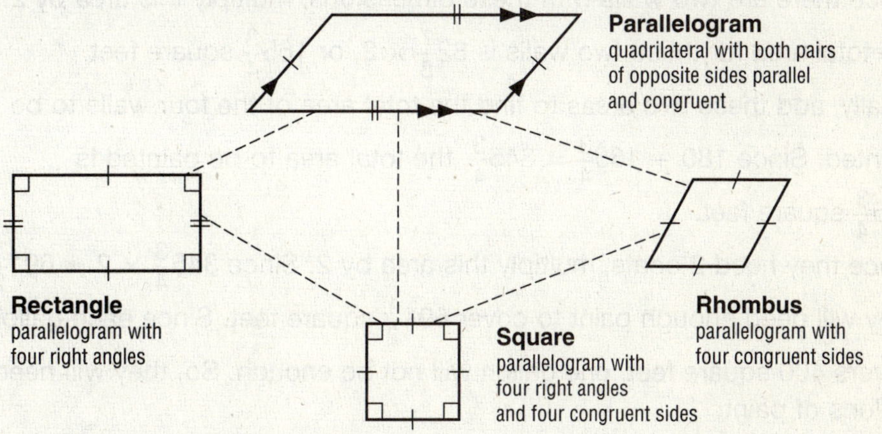

Practice On Your Own, page 18

1. D **2.** G **3.** A **4.** H **5.** C **6.** F **7.** B

Measurement

Volume of Prisms and Cylinders: Shipping Shenanigans, page 22

First, find the volume of the rectangular prism.

$V = \ell wh$	Volume of rectangular prism
$V = 9(6)(8)$	Replace ℓ with 9, w with 6, h with 8.
$V = 432$	Multiply.

So, the volume of the package in the shape of the rectangular prism is 432 in^3.
Next, find the volume of the triangular prism.

$V = Bh$	Volume of prism
$V = \frac{1}{2}(8)(7)(12)$	Replace B with the area of the triangular base, $\frac{1}{2}(8)(7)$, and h with 12.
$V = 336$	Multiply.

So, the volume of the package in the shape of the triangular prism is 336 in^3. Since $432 > 336$, the package in the shape of the rectangular prism (Marta's package) will cost the most to mail.

Area of Polygons: Paint by Number, page 23

First, find the area of the two walls with dimensions 9 feet by 10 feet. The area of one wall with these dimensions is 9×10, or 90 square feet. Since there are two walls with these dimensions, multiply this area by 2. So, the total area for these two walls is 90×2, or 180 square feet.

Next, find the area of the two walls with dimensions $8\frac{1}{2}$ feet by $9\frac{3}{4}$ feet. The area of one wall with these dimensions is $8\frac{1}{2} \times 9\frac{3}{4}$, or $82\frac{7}{8}$ square feet. Since there are two walls with these dimensions, multiply this area by 2. So, the total area for these two walls is $82\frac{7}{8} \times 2$, or $165\frac{3}{4}$ square feet.

Finally, add these two areas to find the total area of the four walls to be painted. Since $180 + 165\frac{3}{4} = 345\frac{3}{4}$, the total area to be painted is $345\frac{3}{4}$ square feet.

Since they need 2 coats, multiply this area by 2. Since $345\frac{3}{4} \times 2 = 691\frac{1}{2}$, they will need enough paint to cover $691\frac{1}{2}$ square feet. Since each gallon covers 400 square feet, one gallon will not be enough. So, they will need two gallons of paint.

Practice On Your Own, page 24

1. C **2.** H **3.** C **4.** G **5.** A **6.** J

Statistics and Probability

Independent Events: Sibling Probabilities, page 28

To have one child, the number of possible outcomes is 2, boy or girl. To have a family of 6 children, the number of possible outcomes is $2 \times 2 \times 2 \times 2 \times 2 \times 2$, or 2^6, or 64. There is only 1 way that all six children will be born boys. So, the probability that all six children will be born boys is $\frac{1}{64}$. You can also arrive at this answer by multiplying $\frac{1}{2} \times \frac{1}{2} \times \frac{1}{2} \times \frac{1}{2} \times \frac{1}{2} \times \frac{1}{2}$, or $\frac{1}{64}$, since the events are independent.

Measures of Central Tendency: Hot! Hot! Hot?, page 29

First, find each of the measures of central tendency.

Mean: $\frac{88 + 90 + 94 + \ldots + 96 + 94 + 93}{30}$, or 90.9

Median: 93

Mode: 94

Either the median or the mode is a good choice to represent the temperatures. The weather forecaster used the mean, 90.9°F or about 91°F, to represent the temperatures. The mean is not appropriate because it is affected by the outliers, 69°F and 68°F. There are only two temperatures below the mean, 88 and 90. The rest of the temperatures are above the mean.

Practice On Your Own, page 30

1. B **2.** H **3.** C **4.** J **5.** B **6.** G

Mathematical Reasoning

Make an Organized List: Cinema Dilemma, page 34

Make an organized list of all the possible ways of arranging the seating order. Place Peter on the end next to the aisle. Make a list of all possible combinations with Peter at the end. Then cross out any combinations that have Miranda on the other end of the row.

~~Peter, Kyla, Lonan, Ramona, Miranda~~
Peter, Kyla, Lonan, Miranda, Ramona
Peter, Kyla, Miranda, Ramona, Lonan
Peter, Kyla, Miranda, Lonan, Ramona
~~Peter, Kyla, Ramona, Lonan, Miranda~~
Peter, Kyla, Ramona, Miranda, Lonan

Peter, Lonan, Kyla, Miranda, Ramona
~~Peter, Lonan, Kyla, Ramona, Miranda~~
Peter, Lonan, Miranda, Ramona, Kyla
Peter, Lonan, Miranda, Kyla, Ramona
Peter, Lonan, Ramona, Sofia, Kyla
~~Peter, Lonan, Ramona, Kyla, Miranda~~

Peter, Ramona, Kyla, Miranda, Lonan
~~Peter, Ramona, Kyla, Lonan, Miranda~~
~~Peter, Ramona, Lonan, Kyla, Miranda~~
Peter, Ramona, Lonan, Miranda, Kyla
Peter, Ramona, Miranda, Lonan, Kyla
Peter, Ramona, Miranda, Kyla, Lonan

Peter, Miranda, Ramona, Kyla, Lonan
Peter, Miranda, Ramona, Lonan, Kyla
Peter, Miranda, Kyla, Ramona, Lonan
Peter, Miranda, Kyla, Lonan, Ramona
Peter, Miranda, Lonan, Kyla, Ramona
Peter, Miranda, Lonan, Ramona, Kyla

Count up the number of possible ways. So, there are 18 possible ways of arranging the teens in the row to watch the movie under these conditions.

Look for a Pattern: Practice Makes Perfect, page 35

The number of shots Alok takes increases by 5 each day. So, tomorrow, Alok will take 25 + 5, or 30 shots. The number of baskets Alok makes increases by 4 each day. So, if the pattern continues, tomorrow, Alok will make 17 + 4, or 21 out of those 30 shots.

Practice On Your Own, page 36

1. D **2.** J **3.** C **4.** H **5.** B **6.** G **7.** B

Number Sense 1: Compare Rational Numbers

I KNOW! COOL, RIGHT? IT'S GOING TO GO RIGHT OVER HERE...
THAT SPACE LOOKS PRETTY SMALL, MAN.
NUKE
FIGHT
ARE YOU SURE IT'LL FIT?
I HADN'T EVEN THOUGHT OF THAT! AND THERE NEEDS TO BE AT LEAST 11 INCHES OF SPACE ON EITHER SIDE OF THE GAME SO WE CAN SERVICE IT!
CALM DOWN. THE SPOT MEASURES $63\frac{15}{16}$ INCHES. HOW BIG IS THE GAME?
LET'S SEE... $41\frac{7}{8}$ INCHES LONG, $28\frac{3}{4}$ INCHES DEEP, AND $71\frac{11}{16}$ INCHES HIGH.
ALL RIGHT...$41\frac{7}{8}$ PLUS 11 INCHES ON THE LEFT, PLUS 11 INCHES ON THE RIGHT IS...
...$63\frac{7}{8}$ INCHES.
...BUT IT NEEDS TO BE LESS THAN OR EQUAL TO $63\frac{15}{16}$ INCHES IN ORDER TO FIT PROPERLY. WILL IT FIT?

Number Sense 1: Compare Rational Numbers (*continued*)

Lucinda and Danvir in:
Fourth and Long
Go Tigers!
How many yards do we have to go again?
Our team has 4 plays to gain a total of 10 yards. If they don't, they lose the ball to the other team.
Oh No! The quarterback went back to pass, but got sacked! We lost 10 yards!
First Down
Yay! The Tigers ran the ball and gained 15 yards! Go Tigers!
Second Down
Third Down
Ugh! They tried to run again and lost 12 yards!
Hooray! A long pass gained them 23 yards!
Fourth Down
Your Turn!
Will the Tigers get to keep the ball?

TRACKING TIME WITH CANDIDA AND MALCOM

PRACTICE On Your Own...

Number Sense

Read each question. Then, fill in the correct answer on the answer document provided by your teacher or on a sheet of paper.

1. Order the set of integers below from least to greatest.

{24, –8, –12, 11, –2}

A {11, 24, –2, –8, –12}
B {24, 11, –2, –8, –12}
C {–2, –8, –12, 11, 24}
D {–12, –8, –2, 11, 24}

2. The world's smallest bird is the bee hummingbird, which is 2.2 inches long. Write this length as a fraction.

F $2\frac{1}{50}$ in.

G $2\frac{1}{5}$ in.

H $2\frac{11}{50}$ in.

J $2\frac{1}{2}$ in.

3. Which number line below best represents $\sqrt{89}$?

A
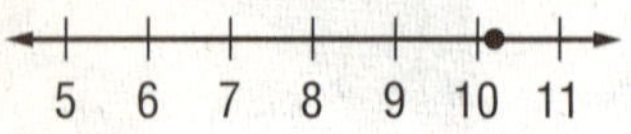

B
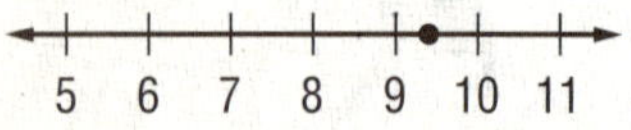

C
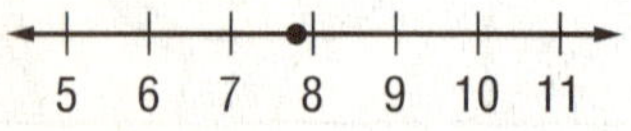

D
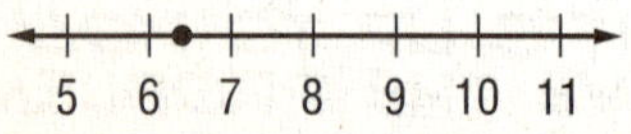

4. How many $3\frac{1}{4}$-inch pieces of ribbon can be cut from a spool containing $19\frac{1}{2}$ inches of ribbon?

F 3 H 6
G 4 J 8

5. A snail travels at a rate of 0.03 miles per hour. At this rate, how far could a snail travel in 1.5 hours?

A 0.045 miles
B 0.45 miles
C 4.5 miles
D 45 miles

6. A group of hikers hiked from Logan's Lake (elevation –25 feet) to Pete's Peak (elevation 432 feet). What is the difference between these elevations?

F –432 feet H 407 feet
G –407 feet J 457 feet

7. Annie paid $7.98 for a six-pack of bottled iced tea. What is the unit price for the iced tea?

A $1.15 per bottle
B $1.33 per bottle
C $1.43 per bottle
D $1.82 per bottle

8. Evaluate the expression below.

$4 + 2(6 - 1) + 5 \cdot 3^2$

F 59 H 45
G 57 J 3

Janelle and Tadeo in:
MISTER LINCOLN GOES SURFING!
Hi-Speed Web Access: 15¢ per minute
Printing: 25¢ per page
Tadeo, aren't you finished yet?
A popular guy like me gets a lot of email!
Well, Mister Popularity, you're taking longer than usual. I think you should hurry up and finish.
Relax, Janelle! I have my good friend President Lincoln here with me!
So, you have $5 to spend today. You've already spent 23 minutes on the Internet and printed 4 pages!
If I don't print any more pages, how much longer can I surf the Internet?

Algebraic Thinking 1: Unit Costs (*continued*)

You have $5.00 total to spend today, so now you have $5.00 - $4.45, or just $0.55 remaining.
At $0.15 per minute, I can still spend another $0.55 ÷ $0.15, or 3.6 minutes on the Internet!
You can't pay for a fraction of a minute, so now you can only spend 3 more minutes on the Internet!
Hmmm...
Since it took us two minutes to solve this problem, could you let me borrow a President Washington to go with my President Lincoln?

ANNIKA, TOMÁS, AND BASHIRA IN
WITS FOR TIPS
THAT LUNCH WAS AWESOME, BASHIRA.
GREAT IDEA TO COME TO YOUR PARENTS' RESTAURANT.
THANKS, GUYS...
I'LL TELL THEM THAT ANNIKA AND TOMÁS APPROVE.
LET'S ESTIMATE THE TOTAL COST OF THE MEAL BEFORE WE GET THE CHECK.
I HAD CHICKEN SHWARMA AND A SODA. THAT COSTS $7.15.
FALAFEL AND A DRINK IS $6.15.
TABOULI AND JUICE COMES TO $5.65.
THAT'S A TOTAL OF $18.95 WITHOUT A TIP.
NOW, WE NEED TO ESTIMATE A 20% TIP.
HERE COMES THE CHECK.
HERE'S YOUR CHECK. HAVE A PLEASANT AFTERNOON.
IS $3.00 ENOUGH FOR THE TIP?
SHOULDN'T IT BE MORE LIKE $5.00?
HOW DO WE FIGURE THIS OUT?
YOUR TURN!
HELP TOMÁS, BASHIRA, AND ANNIKA ESTIMATE A 20% TIP.

Algebraic Thinking 3: Write Equations

PRACTICE On Your Own...

Algebraic Thinking

Read each question. Then, fill in the correct answer on the answer document provided by your teacher or on a sheet of paper.

1. Emma's current allowance is \$12 per week. Each week, she saves 15% of her allowance to deposit into her savings account. How much does she have left each week for spending money?

A \$11.82 **C** \$1.80
B \$10.20 **D** \$0.18

2. Triangle *DEF* is similar to triangle *STU*. What is the value of x?

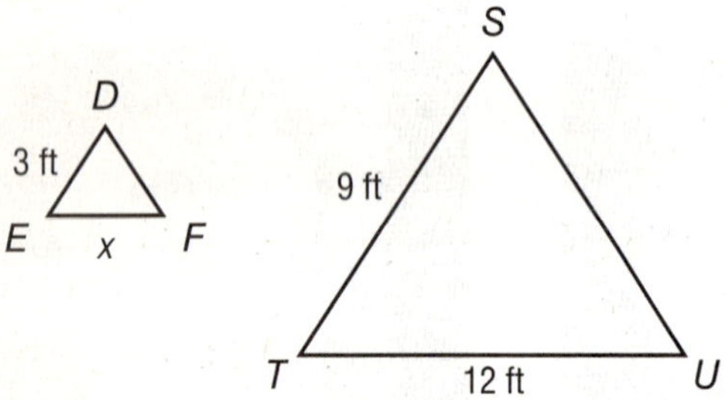

F 4 ft **H** 8 ft
G 6 ft **J** 10 ft

3. Which problem situation represents the equation $g = 2(b) + 4$?

A Brad scored b points. Gabriel scored 2 more than 4 times as many points as Brad. How many points g did Gabriel score?

B Brad scored b points. Gabriel scored 4 more than twice as many points as Brad. How many points g did Gabriel score?

C Gabriel scored g points. Brad scored 4 more points than Gabriel. How many points b did Brad score?

D Gabriel scored g points. Brad scored 2 times as many points as Gabriel. How many points b did Brad score?

4. The Empire State Building is 1,250 feet tall. The Sears Tower is 204 feet taller than the Empire State Building. Which equation could be used to find h, the height in feet of the Sears Tower?

F $1{,}250 = 204h$
G $204 = 1{,}250 + h$
H $1{,}250 = h + 204$
J $h = 1{,}250 + 204$

5. Let n represent a term's position in a sequence. Which algebraic expression can be used to find the nth term in the sequence below?

1, 3, 5, 7, 9, ...

A $n + 1$ **C** $n + 2$
B $2n - 1$ **D** $2n + 1$

6. The graph shows the relationship between the diameter d of a circle and its circumference C.

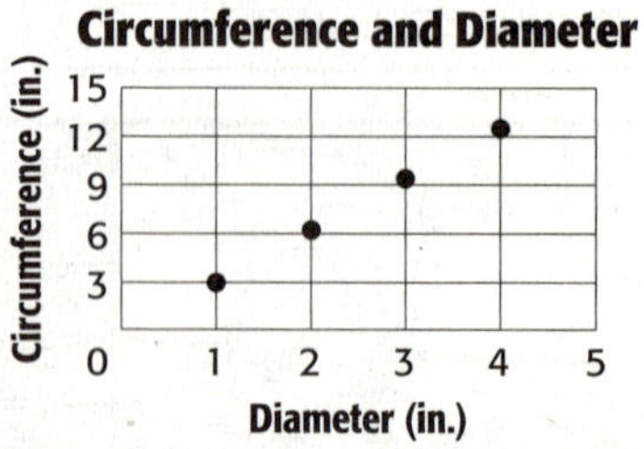

Which equation best represents the data in the graph?

F $C = \pi + d$
G $C = \pi - d$
H $C = \pi d$
J $C = \pi \div d$

LAURA & KEITH IN A TALL STORY
THERE'S NO WAY HE'S 15 FEET TALL, LAURA.
HOW TALL DO YOU THINK HE IS THEN, KEITH?
I'M ESTIMATING NO MORE THAN 10 FEET.
LET'S FIGURE OUT WHO'S CLOSER.
LOSER BUYS THE ICE CREAM!
YOU'RE ON!
FIRST, I'LL MEASURE YOUR SHADOW...4FT.

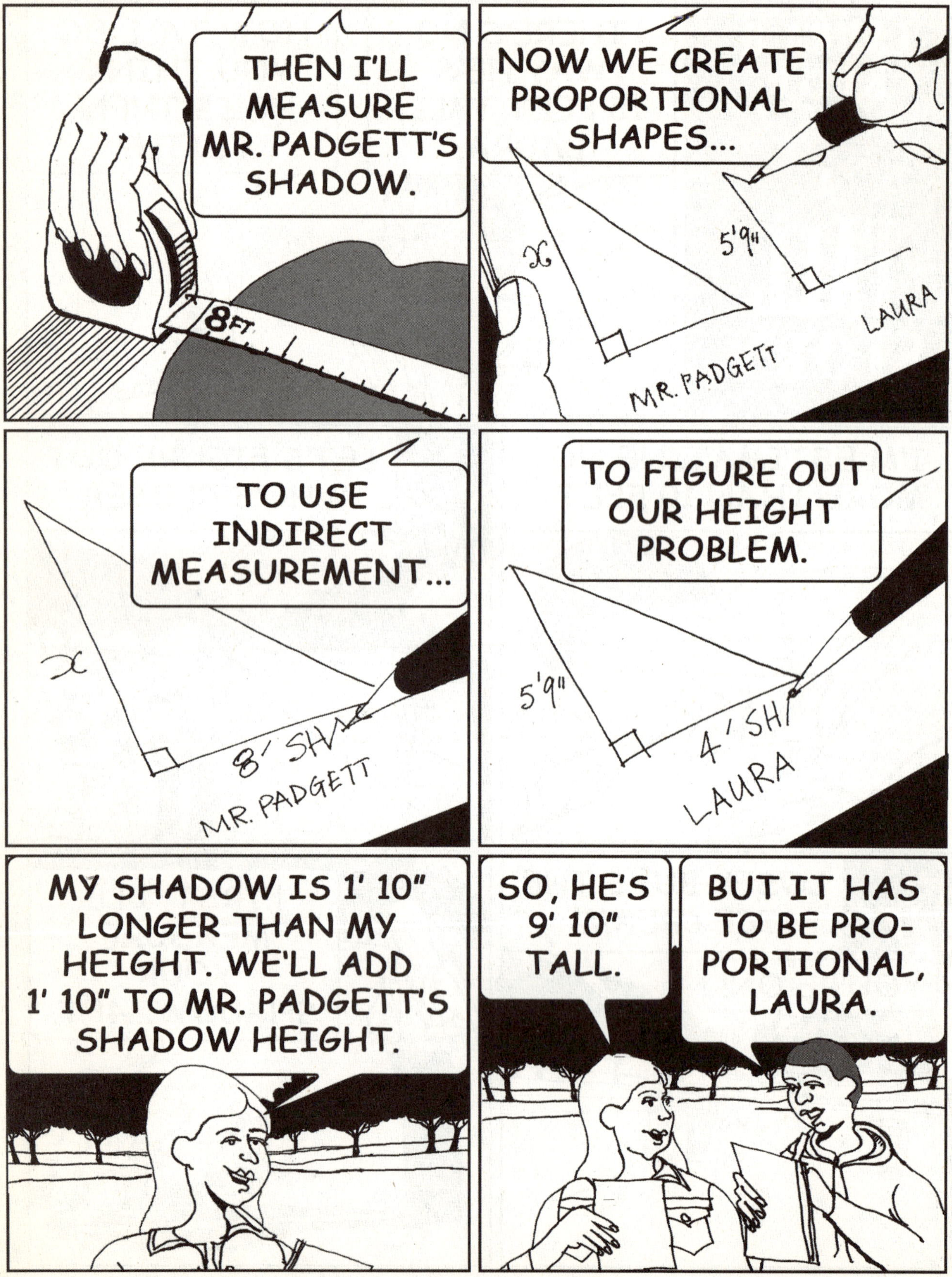
THEN I'LL MEASURE MR. PADGETT'S SHADOW.
8FT
NOW WE CREATE PROPORTIONAL SHAPES...
x
5'9"
MR. PADGETT
LAURA
TO USE INDIRECT MEASUREMENT...
x
8' SH
MR. PADGETT
TO FIGURE OUT OUR HEIGHT PROBLEM.
5'9"
4' SH
LAURA
MY SHADOW IS 1' 10" LONGER THAN MY HEIGHT. WE'LL ADD 1' 10" TO MR. PADGETT'S SHADOW HEIGHT.
SO, HE'S 9' 10" TALL.
BUT IT HAS TO BE PRO-PORTIONAL, LAURA.

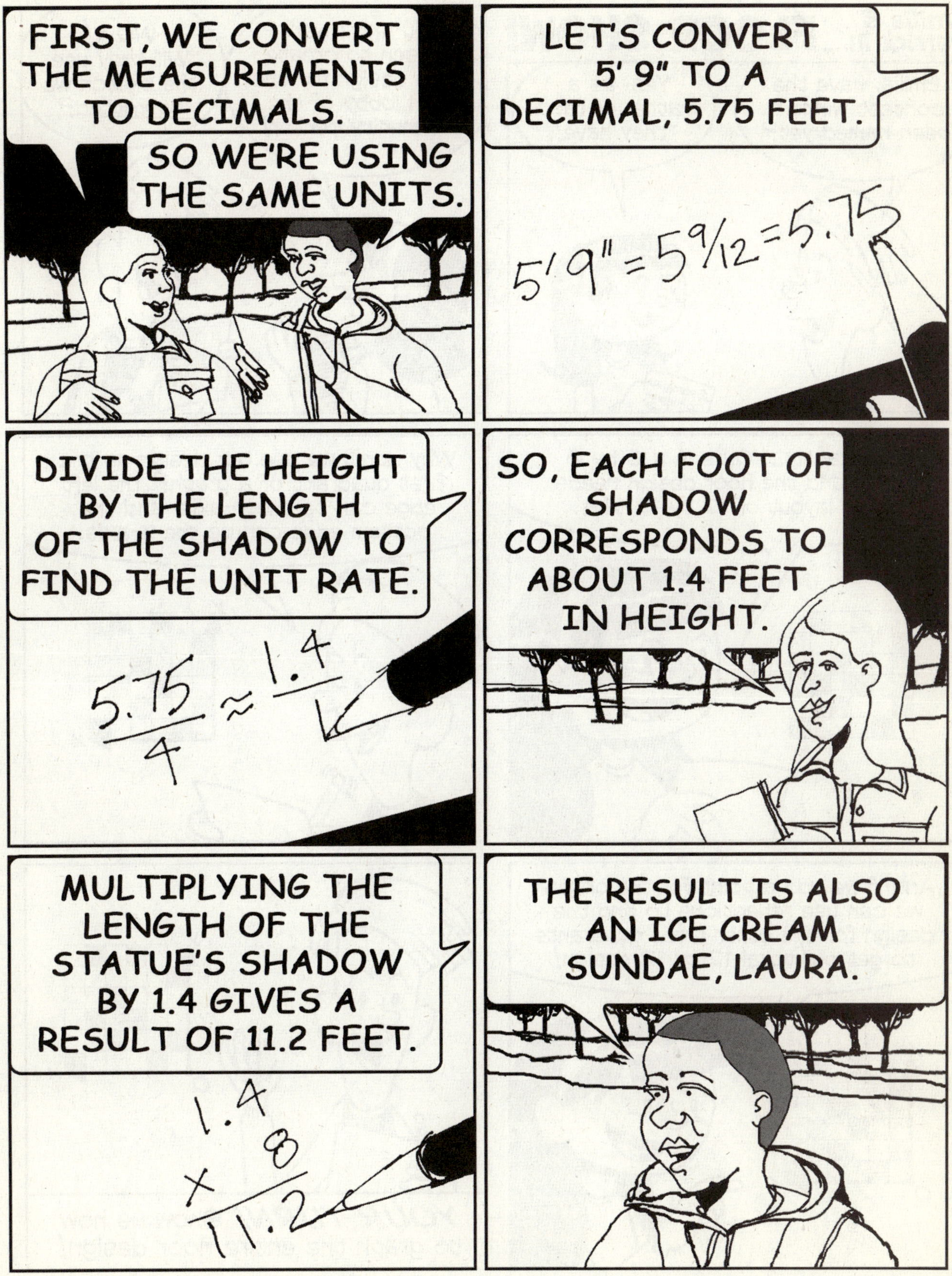
FIRST, WE CONVERT THE MEASUREMENTS TO DECIMALS.
SO WE'RE USING THE SAME UNITS.
LET'S CONVERT 5' 9" TO A DECIMAL, 5.75 FEET.
5' 9" = 5 9/12 = 5.75
DIVIDE THE HEIGHT BY THE LENGTH OF THE SHADOW TO FIND THE UNIT RATE.
5.75/4 ≈ 1.4
SO, EACH FOOT OF SHADOW CORRESPONDS TO ABOUT 1.4 FEET IN HEIGHT.
MULTIPLYING THE LENGTH OF THE STATUE'S SHADOW BY 1.4 GIVES A RESULT OF 11.2 FEET.
1.4
× 8
11.2
THE RESULT IS ALSO AN ICE CREAM SUNDAE, LAURA.

Geometry 2: Reflections

Geometry 3: Quadrilaterals

PRACTICE

On Your Own...

Geometry

Read each question. Then, fill in the correct answer on the answer document provided by your teacher or on a sheet of paper.

1. Which of the following statements is true concerning ∠1 and ∠2 shown?

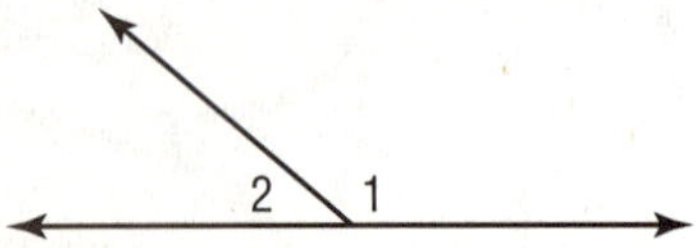

- **A** Both angles are acute.
- **B** Both angles are straight.
- **C** ∠1 and ∠2 are complementary angles.
- **D** ∠1 and ∠2 are supplementary angles.

2. If the point (3, −4) is reflected across the *x*-axis, what will be the coordinates of the point after the reflection?

- **F** (−3, 4)
- **G** (3, 4)
- **H** (−3, −4)
- **J** (0, 0)

3. Triangle *XYZ* has m∠*X* = 108° and m∠*Y* = 22°. What is m∠*Z*?

- **A** 50°
- **B** 68°
- **C** 72°
- **D** 130°

4. A quadrilateral with four congruent sides, opposite sides parallel, and opposite angles congruent is best classified by which of the following terms?

- **F** parallelogram
- **G** rectangle
- **H** rhombus
- **J** trapezoid

5. Which ordered pair names point *P*?

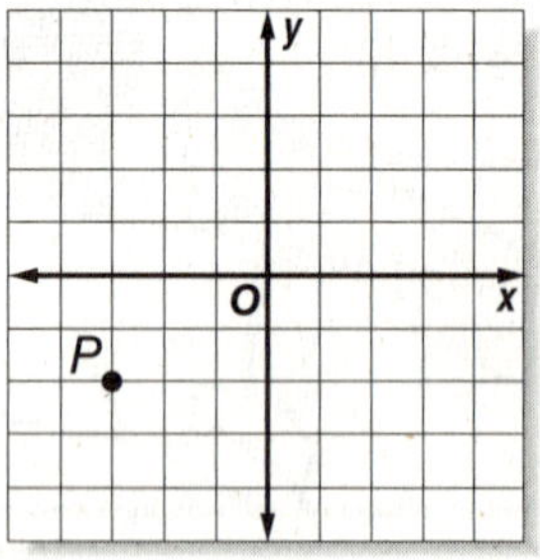

- **A** (−2, −3)
- **B** (−3, 2)
- **C** (−3, −2)
- **D** (2, −3)

6. A triangle with no congruent sides and exactly one right angle is best classified by which of the following terms?

- **F** scalene and right
- **G** scalene and obtuse
- **H** isosceles and right
- **J** equilateral and acute

7. If segment *CD* is translated 2 units right and 4 units down, what will be the coordinates of point *C* and point *D* in their new position?

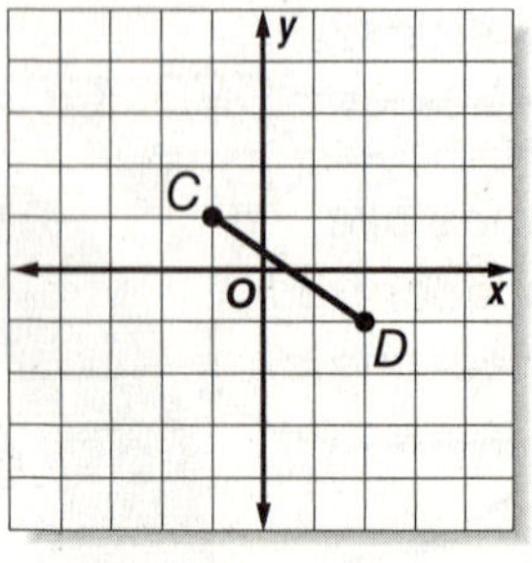

- **A** *C*′(−3, −3), *D*′(0, −5)
- **B** *C*′(1, −3), *D*′(4, −5)
- **C** *C*′(1, 5), *D*′(4, 3)
- **D** *C*′(5, 1), *D*′(3, 4)

Measurement 1: Volume of Cylinders

Measurement 1: *Volume of Cylinders (continued)*

Measurement 1: Volume of Cylinders (*continued*)

Measurement 2: *Volume of Prisms and Cylinders*

Adelina and Jacob in:
Paint by Number
I think we are going to need 2 coats of paint in this room.
Well, I've got a whole gallon of paint.
What?! Just one? That will never be enough!
These two walls are 9 feet across and 10 feet high...
...and these two walls are $8\frac{1}{2}$ feet by $9\frac{3}{4}$ feet.
It says on the label that each gallon will cover 400 square feet.
Your Turn!
Will one gallon be enough for two coats?

PRACTICE

On Your Own...

Measurement

Read each question. Then, fill in the correct answer on the answer document provided by your teacher or on a sheet of paper.

1. Which equation can be used to find the volume of the solid?

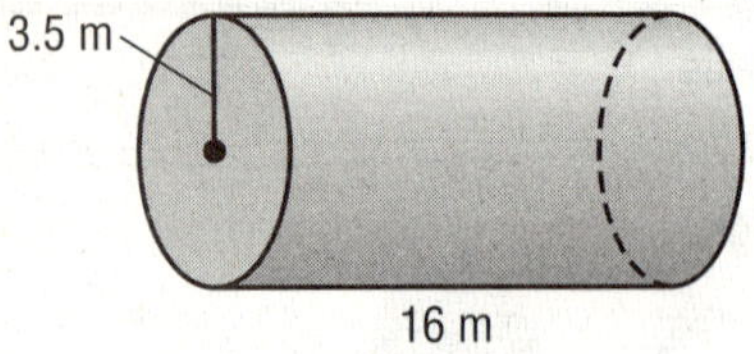

A $V = \pi(8)^2(3.5)$

B $V = \pi(16)^2(3.5)$

C $V = \pi(3.5)^2(16)$

D $V = \pi(7)^2(16)$

2. Find the area of the flag.

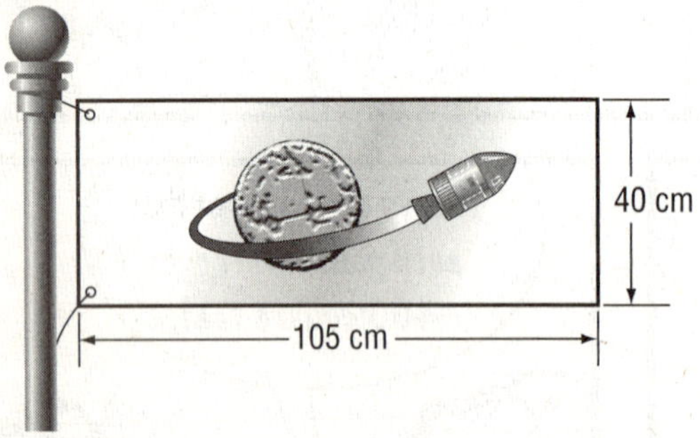

F 290 cm^2 H 4,200 cm^2

G 420 cm^2 J 4,200 cm^3

3. A suitcase is in the shape of a rectangular prism. It is 25 inches long, 18 inches wide, and 8 inches deep. Which equation should be used to find the volume of the suitcase?

A $V = \left(\frac{1}{2} \cdot 18 \cdot 8\right)25$

B $V = \left(\frac{1}{2} \cdot 25 \cdot 18\right)8$

C $V = 25 \cdot 18 \cdot 8$

D $V = 8^2 \cdot 18 \cdot 25$

4. Find the circumference of the pizza. Use 3.14 for π.

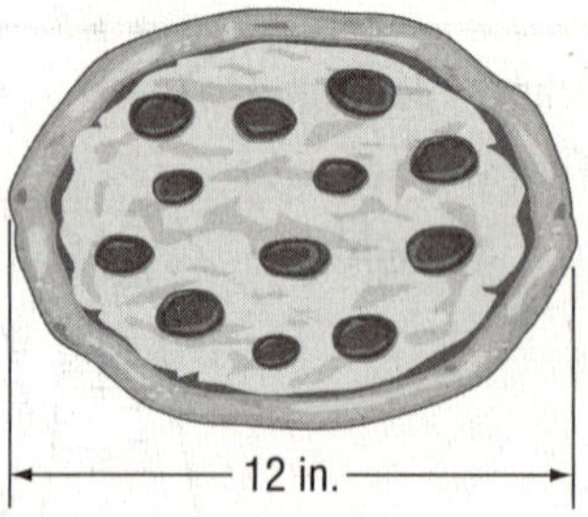

F 18.84 in. H 113.0 in.

G 37.68 in. J 452.2 in.

5. Which of the following would give the best estimate for the volume of a can of juice that is 12.9 centimeters tall with a diameter of 6.08 centimeters?

A $V = \pi(3^2)(13)$ C $V = \pi(6^2)(6)$

B $V = \pi(6^2)(13)$ D $V = \pi(13^2)(6)$

6. Find the volume of the prism below. Round to the nearest tenth.

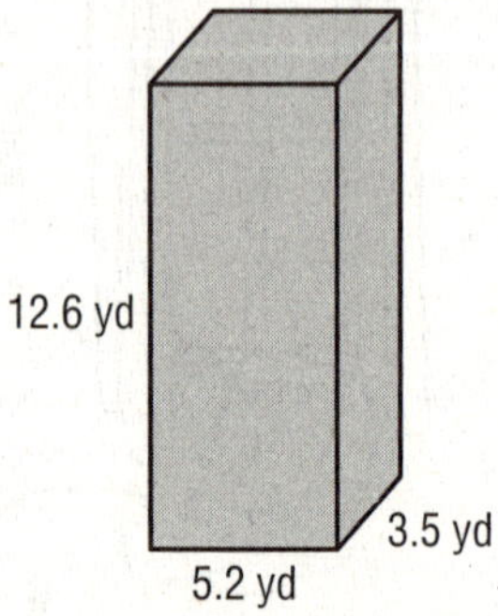

F 21.3 yd^3

G 83.7 yd^3

H 114.7 yd^3

J 229.3 yd^3

Statistics and Probability 1: Probability

LUCKY COUNT with Awenita and Paz

LET'S LIST EACH POSSIBLE OUTCOME.
WE'LL USE **H** FOR HEADS AND **T** FOR TAILS.
T,T,T - ALL THREE TAILS. I WIN.
THREE OUTCOMES OF ONE TAIL, TWO HEADS - T,H,H, - H,H,T - H,T,H. *I* WIN.
THREE OUTCOMES OF TWO TAILS, ONE HEAD - H,T,T - T,T,H - T,H,T. I WIN.
H,H,H - ALL THREE HEADS AND ***YOU LOSE!***

Statistics and Probability 1: Probability (*continued*)

Sibling Probabilities

WITH SKYLER, JORDAN, RUBEN, AND MEI-YIN

Statistics and Probability 3: Measures of Central Tendency

hot! hot! hot?

WITH ISABEL AND ETHAN

PRACTICE On Your Own...

Statistics and Probability

Read each question. Then, fill in the correct answer on the answer document provided by your teacher or on a sheet of paper.

1. An ice cream shop offers a special in which customers can choose a cone or a cup with one scoop of chocolate, vanilla, or strawberry ice cream for $1.50. Which list shows all the possible outcomes?

A

Outcomes	
cone	vanilla
cup	strawberry
cone	chocolate

C

Outcomes	
cup	vanilla
cup	chocolate
cone	strawberry

B

Outcomes	
cone	vanilla
cup	vanilla
cone	chocolate
cup	chocolate
cone	strawberry
cup	strawberry

D

Outcomes	
cone	vanilla
cup	chocolate
cone	strawberry
cone	vanilla
cup	chocolate
cup	strawberry

2. A box contains 3 yellow markers, 4 red markers, and 2 green markers. Another box contains 4 black pens and 6 blue pens. If Marcus chooses a marker and a pen at random, what is the probability that he will choose a red marker and a blue pen?

F $\frac{8}{45}$ **H** $\frac{4}{15}$

G $\frac{3}{15}$ **J** $\frac{10}{19}$

3. Grace's test scores in History are listed below. What is her mean test score?

77, 90, 82, 95, 86, 70, 92, 91, 82

A 25 **C** 85

B 82 **D** 86

4. Isabelle has a collection of 12 DVDs. She chooses a DVD from her set of DVDs at random. Then, she chooses a second DVD from the same set at random without replacing the first DVD chosen. What is the probability that she will select her favorite DVD first and her least favorite DVD second?

F $\frac{1}{12}$ **H** $\frac{1}{121}$

G $\frac{1}{23}$ **J** $\frac{1}{132}$

5. The graph shows the amount earned each year from the annual fund-raiser at Raheem's school. Predict about how much his school will earn from the fund-raiser in 2015 if the trend continues.

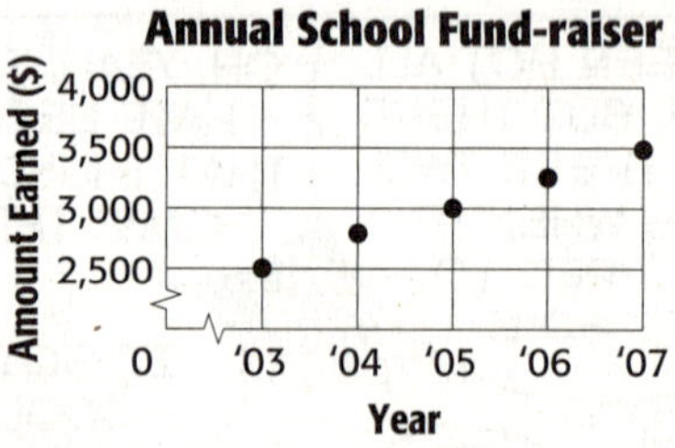

A $6,500 **C** $4,500

B $5,500 **D** $4,000

6. Which measure is best used to describe the center of the data set below?

5, 13, 11, 10, 14, 12, 5, 74

F mean

G median

H mode

J range

Mathematical Reasoning 1: Four-Step Plan

We can figure out what the discount will be, and then add in the sales tax to see exactly how much you'll need.
Tax. I forgot about that. The tax rate is 6.5%.
Don't panic. First let's figure out the discounted price. Then we can add the tax.
10% of $139.99 is about $14. And $139.99-$14 is $125.99.
139.99
x 0.1
13.999
$125.99
Nice. But when we add the tax it's...

Mathematical Reasoning 1: Four-Step Plan (*continued*)

Mathematical Reasoning 2: Make an Organized List

KEISHA, JAMES, AND ALOK IN:
"PRACTICE MAKES PERFECT"
WOW, NICE SHOT, ALOK!
YEAH, YOU'RE GETTING PRETTY GOOD!
THANKS. I'VE BEEN PRACTICING ALL WEEK.
GET THIS: MONDAY, I ONLY MADE 1 OUT OF 5 SHOTS.
ON TUESDAY, I MADE 5 OUT OF 10.
WEDNESDAY, I MADE 9 OUT OF 15.
THEN ON THURSDAY, I MADE 13 OUT OF 20...
...AND TODAY, I MADE 17 OUT OF 25!
WOW. ARE YOU COMING BACK TOMORROW?
YUP.
I WONDER... IF THIS PATTERN CONTINUES, HOW MANY BASKETS WILL HE MAKE TOMORROW?
...AND HOW MANY SHOTS WILL HE TAKE?
YOUR TURN!
NOW IT'S UP TO YOU TO SOLVE THE PROBLEM!
HEY GUYS! DON'T JINX ME!

PRACTICE

On Your Own...

Mathematical Reasoning

Read each question. Then, fill in the correct answer on the answer document provided by your teacher or on a sheet of paper.

1. The circumference of the Earth is about 24,901 miles. Which expression can be used to find the approximate diameter *d* of the Earth?

A $24{,}901 + \pi$ **C** $24{,}901 \times \pi$

B $24{,}901 - \pi$ **D** $24{,}901 \div \pi$

2. What are the next two figures in the pattern shown?

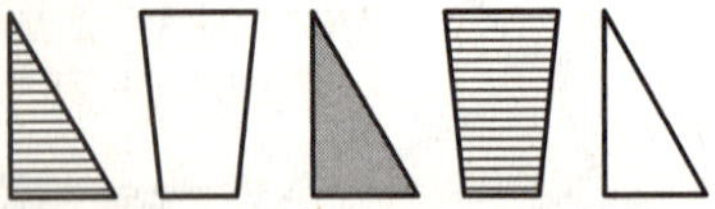

F

H

G

J

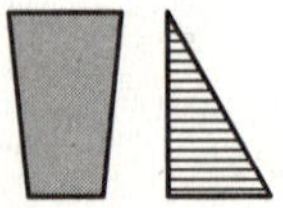

3. A number is multiplied by 5. Then, 4 is subtracted from the product. Finally, the difference is divided by 2. The result is 23. Which of the following equations could be used to find the number *n*?

A $5 + n - 4 = \frac{23}{2}$

B $5n + 4 = 23$

C $\frac{5n - 4}{2} = 23$

D $\frac{5n + 4}{23} = 2$

4. Elena spent $12.50 at dinner. Then, she spent $9.95 at the mall and $15 at the movies. She had $3.65 left. How much did Elena have originally?

F $33.80 **H** $41.10

G $37.45 **J** $42.00

5. Which of the following expressions would best estimate the perimeter *P* in feet of a garden that is 12.15 feet long and 8.89 feet wide?

A $P = 2(12) + 2(8)$

B $P = 2(12) + 2(9)$

C $P = 2(13) + 2(8)$

D $P = 2(13) + 2(9)$

6. The table shows the attendance at a high school marching band pops concert for several years.

Pops Concert	
Year	**Attendance**
2003	586
2004	601
2005	631
2006	676
2007	736

If the trend continues, what will be the attendance in 2010?

F 811

G 1,006

H 1,126

J 1,261

7. Over the summer, Carlos works about 25 hours a week at the library. He earns $8.25 per hour. At this rate, how much will Carlos earn in 7 weeks?

A $2,887.50

B $1,443.75

C $206.25

D $57.75